SYRIA

...in Pictures

Courtesy of UNRWA

Visual Geography Series®

SYRIA

...in Pictures

Prepared by
Geography Department

Lerner Publications Company
Minneapolis

Courtesy of UNRWA

Clutching an Arabic storybook, a young student reads aloud in class.

This book is a newly commissioned title in the Visual Geography Series. The text is set in 10/12 Century Textbook.

LIBRARY OF CONGRESS CATALOGING-IN-PUBLICATION DATA

Syria in pictures / prepared by Geography Department, Lerner Publications Company.
    p. cm. — (Visual geography series)
    Includes index.
    Summary: Describes the topography, history, society, economy, and governmental structure of Syria.
    ISBN 0-8225-1867-8
    I. Syria. [1. Syria.] II. Lerner Publications Company. Geography Dept. III. Series: Visual geography series (Minneapolis, Minn.)
DS93.S955   1990
956.91—dc20   89-13655
                                              CIP
                                               AC

International Standard Book Number: 0-8225-1867-8
Library of Congress Catalog Card Number: 89-13655

VISUAL GEOGRAPHY SERIES ®

Publisher
Harry Jonas Lerner
Associate Publisher
Nancy M. Campbell
Senior Editor
Mary M. Rodgers
Editors
Gretchen Bratvold
Dan Filbin
Phyllis Schuster
Photo Researchers
Karen A. Sirvaitis
Kerstin Coyle
Editorial/Photo Assistant
Marybeth Campbell
Consultants/Contributors
Isaac Eshel
Sandra K. Davis
Designer
Jim Simondet
Cartographer
Carol F. Barrett
Indexers
Kristine S. Schubert
Sylvia Timian
Production Manager
Gary J. Hansen

Independent Picture Service

A Syrian worker breaks up stones to prepare a road for repair.

Acknowledgments

Title page photo by The Hutchison Library.

Elevation contours adapted from *The Times Atlas of the World*, seventh comprehensive edition (New York: Times Books, 1985).

1 2 3 4 5 6 7 8 9 10 99 98 97 96 95 94 93 92 91 90

Near the modern village of Tadmor in central Syria lie the ruins of Palmyra. This city flourished in the third century A.D., until the Romans – one of Syria's many conquerors – destroyed its temples, residences, and roads. Built near an oasis (fertile area), Palmyra was an important stopping point for desert caravans that traveled the width of Syria in ancient times.

Contents

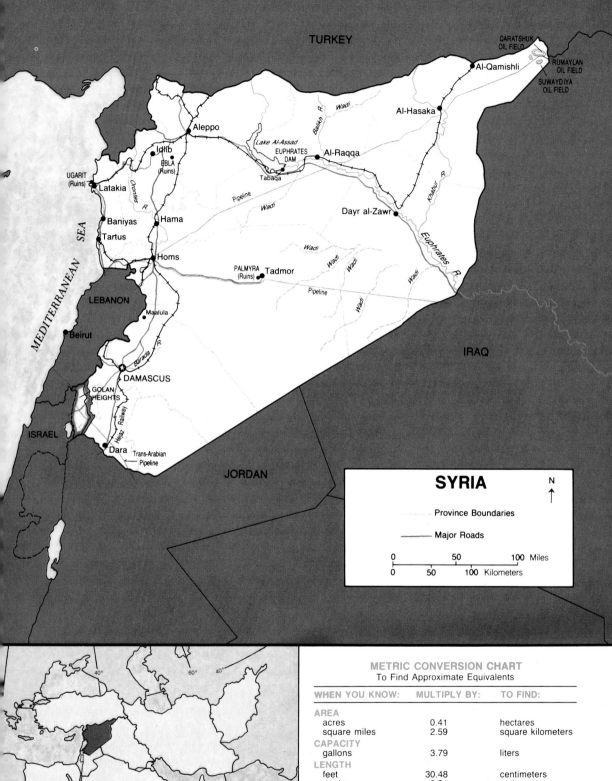

TURKEY

QARATSHUK
OIL FIELD

Al-Qamishli

RUMAYLAN
OIL FIELD

SUWAYDIYA
OIL FIELD

Al-Hasaka

Wadi

Balikh R.

Aleppo

Idlib

EBLA
(Ruins)

Lake Al-Assad

EUPHRATES
DAM

Al-Raqqa

Tabaqa

UGARIT
(Ruins)

Latakia

Orontes R.

Pipeline

Wadi

Khabur R.

Baniyas

Hama

Dayr al-Zawr

Tartus

Euphrates R.

Homs

Wadi

MEDITERRANEAN SEA

PALMYRA
(Ruins)

Tadmor

Wadi

Wadi

Wadi

Wadi

Pipeline

Wadi

LEBANON

Maalula

Beirut

IRAQ

Barada R.

DAMASCUS

GOLAN
HEIGHTS

ISRAEL

Hejaz Railway

Dara

Trans-Arabian
Pipeline

JORDAN

SYRIA

N

‒‒‒‒‒‒ Province Boundaries

——— Major Roads

0   50   100 Miles
0   50   100 Kilometers

MIDDLE EAST
SYRIA

40°

60°

40°

20°

20°

20°

40°

60°

0   500 Miles
0   500 Kilometers

INDIAN OCEAN

METRIC CONVERSION CHART
To Find Approximate Equivalents

WHEN YOU KNOW:	MULTIPLY BY:	TO FIND:
AREA		
acres	0.41	hectares
square miles	2.59	square kilometers
CAPACITY		
gallons	3.79	liters
LENGTH		
feet	30.48	centimeters
yards	0.91	meters
miles	1.61	kilometers
MASS (weight)		
pounds	0.45	kilograms
tons	0.91	metric tons
VOLUME		
cubic yards	0.77	cubic meters
TEMPERATURE		
degrees Fahrenheit	0.56 (*after* subtracting 32)	degrees Celsius

On a street in Damascus, the Syrian capital, a motorcyclist and his passenger cut in front of a colorful bus. Urban populations throughout the nation have increased dramatically in recent years as people move from the countryside in search of jobs.

Introduction

The Syrian Arab Republic, located at the eastern end of the Mediterranean Sea, has long been a site of trade, invasion, and cultural exchange. Among Syria's many conquerors were Greeks, Romans, Arabs, European crusaders, Ottoman Turks, and, in the twentieth century, the French. As a result, the nation has a varied heritage, including Arab and Kurdish ethnic groups and Islamic and Christian religions. This rich combination has led to disunity, as people cling to group loyalties rather than to a national identity.

Syria plays a powerful role in southwestern Asia—a region long known as the Middle East. After achieving independence from France in 1946, Syria united with Egypt for a time. Since the mid-1970s,

Syrian forces have been in Lebanon, and Syrian leaders have tried to control some aspects of Lebanese affairs. In addition, Syria sees itself as the Arab nation most active in opposing the State of Israel, which was created in the Middle East as a Jewish homeland in 1948. Syrian leaders have rejected peace plans that accept Israel's presence in the region.

Since independence, government overthrows have become the usual way to change Syrian administrations. The last takeover occurred in late 1970, when General Hafiz al-Assad seized power. A member of a minority religious sect, Assad has brought nearly 20 years of national stability at the expense of personal and political freedoms. In recent years, economic growth—once a theme of the Assad administration—has slowed because of policies that restrict development and because of heavy military spending.

Unlike many Middle Eastern nations, Syria is not entirely dependent on oil income to sustain itself. The country also has some fertile land. Thus, Syria has strong potential to broaden its economy and to feed its citizens. As Syria enters the 1990s, its economic policies—as well as its relations with neighboring states—will help to determine the nation's long-term well-being.

A farm worker walks along an irrigation canal that provides water for a newly cultivated field in northern Syria.

Syrian soldiers patrolled a street in Sidon, Lebanon, in the mid-1970s, when Syria sent its first troops into the area. Since then, the number of Syrian soldiers in Lebanon has risen to 40,000.

Syrian children learn about their country's eventful past by visiting historic places, such as the Azm Palace in Damascus. Built in the mid-1700s for an Ottoman governor, the palace now houses an art museum.

A section of the Anti-Lebanon Mountains shows the rounded hillsides that help to define the boundary between Lebanon and Syria. The highest mountains rise to about 9,000 feet above sea level, but many of the peaks are much lower.

1) The Land

Syria covers an area of more than 71,000 square miles, making it slightly larger than the state of Oklahoma. Turkey lies to the north, and Iraq is situated to the east. Jordan shares Syria's southern frontier, and the Mediterranean Sea, Lebanon, and Israel border Syria to the west.

The boundary with Israel has been in dispute since 1967. In that year, Israeli forces captured strategic hills in southwestern Syria called the Golan Heights. The Israeli government made them part of Israel in 1981. Syria still claims the Golan Heights as part of its national territory.

Topography

Syria has four natural land features. A north-south group of mountains separates a coastal plain from the interior. East of the mountains lie a fertile plateau and the Syrian Desert.

The country's narrow coastal plain extends for over 70 miles along the Mediterranean Sea between Turkey and Lebanon. North of the Syrian port of Latakia, the shoreline tends to be rugged, with rocky cliffs, while south of the city, the landscape is more level. Because the coastal plain receives adequate rainfall, the land is intensely farmed and densely populated.

Syria's mountains are concentrated in the west and south. Parallel to the coastal strip is the Jabal al-Nusayriya—a limestone range that reaches its highest point, about 5,000 feet, at the northern end of the mountain chain. East of this range lies the Great Rift Valley (also called the Al-Ghab Depression), through which the Orontes River flows. A giant crack in the earth's crust created this trenchlike valley, which extends southward far into the African continent. South of the Jabal al-Nusayriya is a narrow corridor—the Homs Gap—which has long been a pathway for traders and invaders.

On the other side of the gap are the Anti-Lebanon Mountains, which mark the

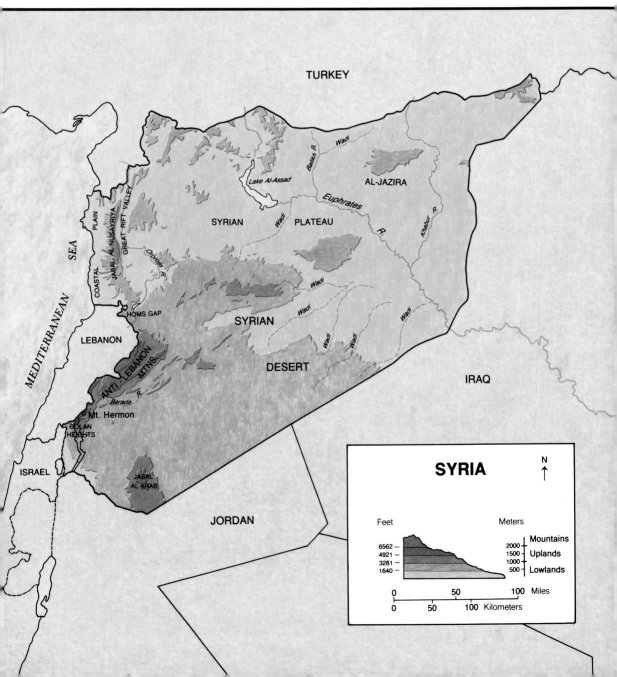

boundary between Lebanon and Syria. The highest peak in this chain—and in Syria—is Mount Hermon (9,232 feet), which lies on the border between the two countries. The Anti-Lebanon Mountains gradually decrease in elevation until they reach the Golan Heights. In the southwest are the volcanic peaks of the Jabal al-Arab (formerly the Jabal Druze). The western slopes of these mountains receive enough rainfall to support cultivated plots. Many Syrians who belong to the Druze religious sect live in this rocky area.

Eastern Syria consists chiefly of a grassy plateau and the Syrian Desert. Irrigation allows farmers to raise much of Syria's food and livestock on the plateau, which has an average elevation of 2,000 feet. Most of the nation's farmers work in this region. The Euphrates River (called Al-Furat in Syria) flows through the northeastern section of the plateau. The waterway helps to create Al-Jazira—the upper part of the Tigris-Euphrates River Valley, which stretches into Iraq.

The Euphrates also forms the northeastern boundary of the Syrian Desert, which extends into Iraq and Jordan. A roughly triangular land feature, the desert reaches an average elevation of 2,000 feet above sea level. Syria's section—which covers most of the nation's southeastern territory—is largely flat and gently slopes toward the Euphrates. Deep *wadis* (riverbeds that carry water only during the rainy season) cut through the desert and also lead to the Euphrates.

Rivers

The Euphrates and the Orontes rivers are Syria's most important waterways. The 2,235-mile-long Euphrates flows from its source in Turkey through a broad stretch of Syria. Eventually the waterway travels through Iraq to the Persian Gulf. As it winds through Syria, the river irrigates farmland and receives the volume of two branch rivers—the Balikh and the Khabur. Plans are in progress to harness these

Courtesy of Bill Hendricks

Members of a nomadic family group, these Bedouin women and children herd sheep and live in woven tents in the Syrian Desert.

Photo by Christine Osborne

With the help of the Soviet government, Syria built the Euphrates Dam in the 1970s. It harnesses the flow of the Euphrates River, which begins in Turkey and ends in Iraq. As it winds through Syria, the waterway also irrigates farmland. Low rainfall and disputes with Turkey and Iraq over use of the river's water have hampered the dam's ability to produce electricity.

waterways for hydropower. The huge Euphrates Dam at Tabaqa redirects water to thousands of acres of once-uncultivated land. This engineering feat also created Lake Al-Assad—a 30-mile-long reservoir.

The 355-mile-long Orontes River begins near Baalbek, Lebanon, and enters Syria south of the city of Homs. Dams at Homs and Hama have rechanneled the Orontes to irrigate the surrounding countryside. As a result of the Orontes River, harvests in western Syria are abundant, and local industries have hydropower to run their operations. After passing through northwestern Syria, the river enters Turkey and then empties into the Mediterranean Sea.

One other river—the Barada—is of importance to Syria. Beginning in the Anti-Lebanon Mountains, the Barada flows through the capital city of Damascus to the desert. The river provides water to the Al-Ghuta Oasis, a fertile area where the capital stands. Although it becomes a mere trickling stream in the dry season, the Barada has allowed Damascus to be inhabited for thousands of years.

Climate

The climate of Syria varies greatly from west to east. Population centers and crop farming occur in places where rainfall is plentiful or where irrigation projects exist. In dry zones, nomads commonly raise livestock.

Although Mediterranean breezes cool the coastal plain, summers (May through August) in this region are generally hot and humid, with temperatures in the eighties and nineties. In winter (November through February), temperatures along the coast range between 48° and 68° F.

13

Syria's highest elevations get snow in winter. Here, several feet of the white powder cover a rural settlement in the Jabal al-Nusayriya.

Jabal al-Nusayriya and the Anti-Lebanon Mountains act as a wall to moisture-carrying winds that blow in from the Mediterranean. As a result, the western slopes of these ranges are wetter and cooler than the eastern elevations. Readings in the western mountains average about 72° F in summer and 40° F in winter. At the highest altitudes, temperatures frequently drop below freezing in the winter.

East of the mountains, the plateau is semi-arid, with hot summers and cool winters. Temperatures can climb to 104° F in the summer, and winter levels fall to the low forties. The desert is the nation's hottest and driest region. In summer, temperatures rise as high as 110° F, and hot winds cause sandstorms that kick up enough dust and sand both to block vision and to rearrange the sand dunes. Winter temperatures in the desert drop to about 35° F.

Syria's wet season lasts from November to March. Rainfall is heaviest along the coast and in the mountain ranges that flank the coastal strip. In these areas, annual precipitation varies from 20 to 40 inches and may exceed 50 inches in some places. The highest elevations receive a portion of their moisture as snow.

Because the mountains keep most of the rain from entering the interior, the rest of Syria is nearly dry. The plateau that lies east of the mountains annually receives about 10 inches of rain. The desert may average as little as 3 inches per year, or in very dry periods, it may not receive any precipitation at all.

Flora and Fauna

Syrians have so thoroughly cleared the coastal plain for farming and housing that not much of the original vegetation survives. Scrubby Mediterranean plants, such as tamarisk and buckthorn, grow in wasteland areas, and bright wildflowers thrive as weeds in cultivated fields.

Forests of oak and pine flourish in the northern part of the Jabal al-Nusayriya, and hardwood trees cover the southern part of the same range. Thin stands of oak, pine, cedar, and cypress survive in the upper elevations of the Anti-Lebanon Mountains. On the grassy plains, terebinth trees are common. A member of the sumac family, this tree is an ancient source of turpentine (a resin used as a paint solvent).

Human settlement patterns have also decreased the habitats of Syria's wild mammals. Nevertheless, deer and gazelles continue to live in remote areas. Rodents —such as dormice, squirrels, and rats—

Courtesy of Mohamed Al-Roumi/Syrian Ministry of Tourism

The small village of Maalula lies about 30 miles north of Damascus at an altitude of more than 5,000 feet. The village's dwellings, as well as its convents and churches, cling to the limestone rock of the Anti-Lebanon Mountains.

Courtesy of Nasri Akil/Syrian Ministry of Tourism

Brilliantly blossoming plants decorate the exterior of the Azm Palace in Damascus.

15

Camels are well suited to desert life in Syria because they can travel many days without water. The animals also get moisture and other nourishment from plants, and their humps store these resources as fat. Camels convert the fat into energy when food and water are scarce. As the animals use up the stored fat, their humps shrink until food and rest restore them to their normal shape.

Courtesy of United Nations

also make their homes in Syria. Other small mammals include hares, hedgehogs, wildcats, weasels, and foxes. Lions and leopards once roamed Syria, but bears are the only large mammals still reported. Among native birds are hawks, kites, cormorants, pelicans, flamingos, cuckoos, and woodpeckers. Desert animals include lizards and chameleons, as well as the sheep and camels of nomadic herders.

Natural Resources

Petroleum is Syria's most important natural resource, but the nation's oil deposits are small compared to those of some other Middle Eastern states. First discovered in Syria in 1957, petroleum is now a leading national export. Most of the country's oil fields lie in eastern Syria.

After oil, Syria's chief resources are natural gas, phosphates, iron ore, salt, and asphalt. Supplies of these substances exist in large enough quantities to be mined profitably. Smaller amounts of coal, copper, lead, and gold have been discovered in mountain areas.

Major Cities

Most of Syria's population live in the western part of the country, where rainfall

Independent Picture Service

Huge storage tanks at Homs contain some of Syria's refined petroleum. Oil is the country's main source of foreign income.

In downtown Damascus stands the Place of the Martyrs, which commemorates the deaths of Arab nationalists in 1916. The bronze column is decorated with electric cables and honors the opening of the first Middle Eastern telegraphic link, which stretched between Damascus and Saudi Arabia.

is relatively plentiful. About half of the nation's 12 million people reside in urban areas. Syria's cities and towns have long histories and feature narrow streets, ancient buildings, and traditional ways of life. Most large urban centers have added modern housing and business districts to accommodate their growing populations.

DAMASCUS

With 1.2 million people, Damascus—the nation's capital and largest city—is Syria's hub of business, government, and communications. Situated between the Anti-Lebanon Mountains and the Syrian Desert, Damascus lies in the Al-Ghuta Oasis—a triangular network of irrigation canals fed by the Barada River.

Located along the route between Europe, the Middle East, and eastern Asia, Damascus has been a trading center since ancient times. In fact, some authorities claim that it is one of the oldest continuously inhab-

ited cities in the world. The capital's streets are crowded with people, trucks, cars, and buses. Merchants sell food, fabrics, and metalwork in markets called *suqs*.

Among the landmarks of ancient Damascus, which lies on the southern bank of the Barada River, is the Umayyad Mosque. One of the most famous houses of worship in the Middle East, the mosque was constructed in A.D. 705 on the site of a former Christian church. The Azm Palace, located near the Umayyad Mosque, was built for an eighteenth-century governor. Also close to the mosque is the tomb of Saladin, a twelfth-century Arab general who defeated European invaders intent on holding the city.

Modern Damascus extends north of the Barada and boasts wide avenues, large apartment buildings, and tall office complexes. The business district took shape during the early 1900s, when France controlled Syria. Many institutions—such as

Sunlight bathes part of Damascus, giving the capital a warm, yellow glow. The old sections of the city remain remarkably unchanged despite thousands of years of habitation. In the background is the Umayyad Mosque, an Islamic house of prayer originally founded in the early eighth century.

the National Museum and the National Library—preserve Syria's cultural diversity. The capital's manufacturing sector produces textiles and processed food. The University of Damascus sits on the outskirts of the capital.

ALEPPO

Located in northwestern Syria, Aleppo—the second largest city in Syria—has over one million inhabitants. Like Damascus, Aleppo has a long, colorful past. Archaeological evidence suggests that people may have settled in the area before 5000 B.C.

Among Aleppo's numerous historic and religious sites is a large, twelfth-century Arab fort. Standing on a bluff that dominates the older part of the city, the fort has beautiful tiled ceilings and strong walls. Shops that offer a wide variety of goods line Aleppo's vast network of suqs. Included in the trading district are traditional public baths and *khans*—ancient resting places for caravan travelers.

Modern Aleppo is a commercial and industrial hub and a marketplace for farmers from surrounding regions. The city's chief industries are textile manufacturing and food processing, mainly of dried fruits, nuts, and tobacco. The Euphrates Dam—which has enabled local farmers to grow large amounts of wheat, barley, and cotton—has increased Aleppo's importance.

Secondary Urban Centers

Homs, with 430,000 people, lies along a route between Damascus and Aleppo in west central Syria. Situated on the Orontes River, the city was once the center of the worship of Baal, a sun god of ancient times. Set amid one of the most fertile areas of Syria, Homs is famous for silk manufacturing and contains large oil-refining facilities.

Hama (population 200,000) was settled long before 1000 B.C. Built on the banks of the Orontes River, the city lies about 30 miles north of Homs in a district where farmers plant large fields of grain and cotton. Hama also contains ancient waterwheels that pump water for irrigation from the Orontes to nearby farmland. Dating from the sixteenth century, some of these devices are 90 feet in diameter. The city's main industries are food processing and the manufacture of clothing and carpets. Hama's oldest sections were destroyed during fighting between an Islamic group and the Syrian army in 1982.

Latakia (population 240,000), the chief seaport of Syria, outlasted the rule of

Courtesy of Nasri Akil/Syrian Ministry of Tourism

In Aleppo, Syria's second largest city, an aerial view of the Citadel shows its dominating position on the cityscape. Built in the thirteenth century, this Arab fortress has withstood earthquakes and Mongol attacks.

The port facilities at Latakia allow a variety of ships to berth at its docks along the Mediterranean Sea. The city also contains ancient Roman ruins and a new university.

Phoenicians, Assyrians, Babylonians, Greeks, and Romans over many centuries. The city's Roman ruins, which include the Temple of Bacchus and the Triumphal Arch, are among the finest ancient sites in Syria. As a result of its seaside location, Latakia benefits from Mediterranean breezes that soften the extremes of the region's summer and winter temperatures. The hub of the Syrian tobacco industry, Latakia also exports cotton, asphalt, and foodstuffs. A leading resort, the city draws visitors to its beaches and historical sites.

These huge wheels—called *norias*—at Hama bring up water from the Orontes River to irrigate nearby farmland. Constructed in the 1500s, the waterwheels pump the water in a slow, churning motion.

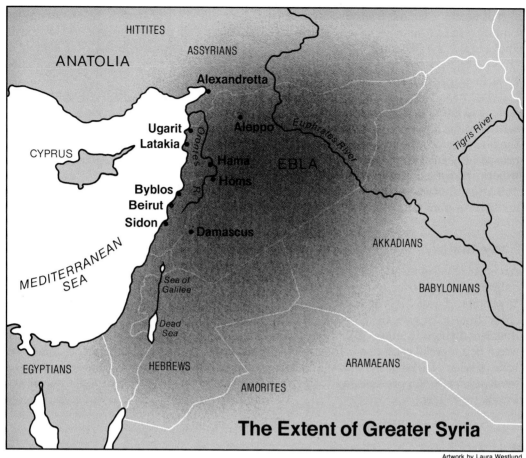

The Extent of Greater Syria

Artwork by Laura Westlund

For thousands of years, the land called Greater Syria covered a large portion of the Middle East and attracted many ancient peoples. Greater Syria's territory stretched into what are now Israel, Jordan, Lebanon, Iraq, and Turkey, as well as into the modern Syrian Arab Republic. (Boundaries reflect current borders.)

2) History and Government

The ancient territory named Greater Syria once included a much larger area than does the modern Syrian Arab Republic. At different times in history, parts of what are now Turkey and Iraq—as well as all of Lebanon, Jordan, and Israel—belonged to Greater Syria.

Nomadic herders lived in the region as early as 5000 B.C. Almost all of these inhabitants were Semitic peoples, whose ancestors originated in the Arabian Peninsula to the south and who shared a common language. Later, Greater Syria's rich farmland drew many other groups to the area.

In time, Greater Syria became a thriving center for agricultural and commercial activity. Builders from as far away as

Egypt used the timber from Syria's mountain forests to construct palaces, temples, and ships. Syria's coastal location attracted traders from all over the Middle East in large numbers.

Lying near the intersection of Africa, Asia, and Europe, Syria became an important trading hub. Whoever could control the flow of goods through the region would prosper. Because of this potential for great wealth, Syria's history involves peoples and kingdoms who struggled against one another to dominate the territory.

Early History

Archaeological evidence of Syria's early inhabitants comes from a site at Ebla. Excavations of this city in northern Syria show that a large-scale Semitic culture flourished there in about 2500 B.C. Ebla was a commercial center that linked Anatolia (modern Turkey), the Tigris-Euphrates River Valley (in present-day Iraq), and Persia (now Iran).

For several centuries, Ebla struggled against Akkad—a kingdom in the southern Tigris-Euprates Valley—for control of the region's trade routes. In about 2250 B.C., the Akkadian king, Naram-Sin, defeated the armies of Ebla and burned the city to the ground.

Meanwhile, a Semitic people called the Amorites had arrived from the Arabian Peninsula in 2400 B.C. In time, they also felt the power of Naram-Sin's forces. Despite his attacks, the Amorites stayed in the region. A branch of this people, the Canaanites, eventually occupied Greater Syria's portion of the Mediterranean coast (present-day Lebanon).

The area's residents developed into expert shipbuilders and sailors, and their activities linked Syria to many new Mediterranean trading centers. By about 1800 B.C., the people became known as Phoenicians—a name taken from the expensive purple dye they made from sea mollusks found in the Mediterranean. One of the main Phoenician cities was Ugarit, located

This golden bowl comes from the ruins of Ugarit, an ancient Phoenician site in northwestern Syria. Ugarit maintained commercial ties with Egypt and Greece and flourished as a trading center between the sixteenth and thirteenth centuries B.C. The bowl depicts hunters in chariots chasing their prey. Charioteers, called *maryannu,* were well-respected members of Ugarit society and passed down their skills to their sons.

Photo by Hirmer Photo Archive

Found at Ugarit, this small clay rod carries the pictorial alphabet that came into use throughout Greater Syria.

north of Latakia. The Phoenicians also contributed to the invention of an alphabet that later came into use throughout the region.

NEW FOREIGN INFLUENCES

The Egyptians and the Hittites (a people from Anatolia) extended control over portions of Syria at various times during the next several hundred years. Two other Semitic peoples—the Hebrews and the Aramaeans—became influential toward the end of the eleventh century B.C.

The Hebrews introduced the region's people to the religious idea of belief in one god. The Aramaeans established themselves as merchants, making Damascus a center for overland commercial routes to southern Arabia and Persia. As Aramaean traders traveled in the Middle East, they spread their language—Aramaic—throughout the area. Aramaic, which used the alphabet that the Phoenicians had developed earlier, became the principal language of Syria.

Between the eleventh and the sixth centuries B.C., Syria was controlled for brief periods by the Assyrians from the north, by the Babylonians from the south, and by the Egyptians from the southwest. From the sixth to the fourth centuries B.C., the land was part of the Persian Empire, un-til Alexander the Great and his Greek armies conquered that vast realm in 333 B.C. When Alexander died in 323, his kingdom broke apart, and Syria came under the authority of one of his generals, named Seleucus.

Photo by Robin Constable/The Hutchison Library

Narrow roads lead to the village of Maalula in western Syria. Hard for outsiders to reach, this long-inhabited place became a stronghold of ancient Christians. Their descendants continue to follow an old form of the Catholic faith and to speak Aramaic—the ancient language of Syria.

A silver tetradrachm coin—issued in 323 B.C., the year Alexander the Great died—shows the head of Hercules *(top)* on the front. The back *(bottom)* depicts Zeus (the strongest of the Greek gods) holding a royal scepter and an eagle. The Greek lettering translates as "Alexander the king." After Alexander's death, his general Seleucus controlled Syria.

This Roman road is among the evidence of Syria's Roman occupation, which lasted from the first century B.C. to the seventh century A.D. Well-made and sturdy, the road is near the town of Idlib in northwestern Syria. Nearby are the ruins of Ebla, a settlement that predates the Roman period.

Seleucus founded a family of rulers known as the Seleucid dynasty, which governed Syria for three centuries. The Seleucid leaders made their capital in Damascus and brought elements of Greek culture to Syria. The Syrians combined Greek ideas with their own learning to make advances in science, architecture, and philosophy. During this period, the Syrians built many roads and cities—including Latakia, named after Seleucus's mother—and traders established commercial routes into Europe and India.

The Romans

In the first century B.C., the Armenians and the Parthians—peoples from the north and east—began to expand their holdings by invading Syrian territory. These groups did not control the region for long, however. In 64 B.C., the Romans—under General Pompey—added Syria to the Roman Empire, which was based in Italy.

The period of Roman rule in Syria was generally prosperous. Roman administrators built roads, temples, and aqueducts (troughs that carry water over long distances). Damascus remained prominent under Roman rule, and the city became famous for its architecture and its schools of law and medicine.

Another flourishing Syrian city was Palmyra (near modern Tadmor), the capital of a powerful semi-independent kingdom that reached its height in the third century A.D. Palmyra was a trading center for caravans as they made their way from Homs to settlements along the Euphrates River. Because the Palmyrenes refused to obey Roman rule, the Romans destroyed the city in A.D. 272.

The extensive ruins of Palmyra cover a wide section of the desert in central Syria. Pillars lined Palmyra's main street, at the end of which stood the Temple of Bel *(top)*. Musical and dramatic entertainments drew Palmyrenes to the theater *(right)*.

25

In A.D. 395, to ease the management of its vast holdings, the Roman Empire split into eastern and western portions. Syria became part of the Eastern Roman (or Byzantine) Empire. Emperors governed the territory from the city of Constantinople (now Istanbul, Turkey). The empire's rulers, who followed the Christian religion, tried to convert the Syrians but were successful only in the northern part of the country.

During the next 240 years, the Byzantine Empire was often at war with Persia over land. Syria frequently became a battlefield, and the fighting financially drained Constantinople. Eventually, the Byzantine rulers stopped paying Arab clans from southern Syria for the border protection that they had provided. With-

out these Arab troops, the empire's southern defenses weakened. Invaders from the Arabian Peninsula met little resistance as they moved toward southern Syria in the early 600s.

Islam and the Arabs

In the early seventh century, an Arab religious leader named Muhammad started a new, one-god faith called Islam. By 629 the followers of Islam—called Muslims—set out from their capital at Mecca in the Arabian Peninsula to establish Islam in other lands. Soon after the death of Muhammad in 632, Muslims divided into two main sects. Sunni Muslims favored electing a leader, while Shiites wanted Islam's head to be chosen from among

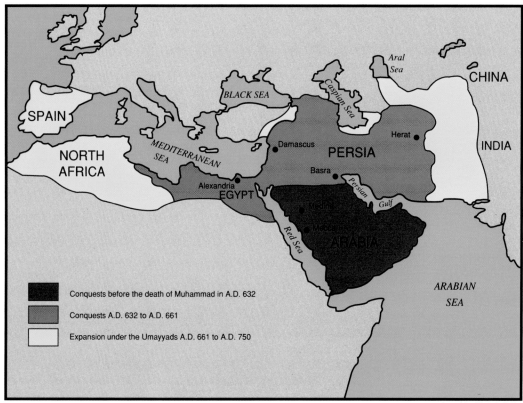

Conquests before the death of Muhammad in A.D. 632

Conquests A.D. 632 to A.D. 661

Expansion under the Umayyads A.D. 661 to A.D. 750

Artwork by Mindy A. Rabin

In A.D. 636, Islamic armies conquered Damascus and made it the first capital of the Islamic Empire. The city grew in importance under the Umayyad dynasty (family of rulers), who brought parts of Asia, Africa, and Europe under Islamic control.

Muhammad's family. The Sunni sect became Islam's dominant group.

Led by Khalid ibn al-Walid, the Arab Muslims conquered Damascus in 636. Under Muslim rule, Syria slowly adopted Islam as the official religion of the country. Muawiya, a Sunni who belonged to the Umayyad family, became the caliph, or ruler, of Syria. In 661 a majority of the faithful elected him the leader of all Muslims, and he chose Damascus as the political capital of Islam.

The city enjoyed a period of fame and wealth as the hub of the Islamic Empire, which Muawiya I and other Umayyad caliphs extended west to Spain and east to central Asia. Under the influence of Islam, Syrians substituted Arabic for Aramaic as the main language of the Middle East. The Umayyads built roads, founded hospitals, and encouraged education. Scholars from other lands studied in Damascus, developing new medical practices and philosophical ideas.

Despite these advances, the empire had unstable leadership, and later Umayyad caliphs fell away from Islamic traditions. In 715 the Abbasids, a rival Muslim family, overthrew the Umayyad dynasty. The Abbasids transferred the capital of the empire from Damascus to Baghdad (in present-day Iraq).

Muslim nobles often challenged Abbasid rule. For example, Sayf al-Dawla Abu al-Hasan ibn Hamdan established the Hamdanid kingdom at Aleppo in the tenth century. Besides defying the authority of the Abbasids in Baghdad, Sayf al-Dawla —who was himself a poet—made Aleppo a center of culture.

Seljuks and Crusaders

In time, the Abbasids also ignored Islamic traditions, and their power over the Islamic Empire weakened. When the Seljuk Turks invaded the region in the late eleventh century, Arab nobles had already split Syria into small Islamic states. The

Photo by Drs. A. A. M. van der Heyden, Naarden, the Netherlands

Among the most important sites in the Middle East, the Umayyad Mosque helped to establish Damascus as a center of Islamic learning and culture in the 700s. Within the mosque's inner courtyard is a small structure raised on several columns. It may once have served as a treasury for public funds.

Seljuks, who had adopted Islam in the tenth century, conquered Syria and established two provinces—one with its capital at Aleppo and the other centered in Damascus.

The Muslim Seljuks also pushed into the territory still controlled by the Eastern Roman Empire in Anatolia. The Seljuks made it difficult for European Christians to pass through Anatolia on their way to Palestine—a Middle Eastern land that both Christians and Muslims considered sacred. To make safe passage possible and to gain riches, Christian armies arrived from western Europe in the late eleventh century.

Known as crusaders, these Christian soldiers sought to control Palestine. They conquered Seljuk territory and set up domains that were centered at Antioch (in Anatolia), Tripoli (in Greater Syria), and

Invading Christian soldiers—called crusaders—built Le Crac des Chevaliers in northwestern Syria as a stronghold against Islamic armies. Completed in the late 1100s, this crusader castle was part of a European effort to seize the Holy Land (a Middle Eastern territory sacred to Christians). The area was also honored by Muslims (followers of Islam). Located on the route between Homs and Tripoli (now in Lebanon), the castle was taken by the Muslim general Saladin in 1187.

Jerusalem (in Palestine). The Syrian cities of Damascus, Homs, and Hama, however, remained under Seljuk authority.

In the early 1100s, constant warfare against the crusaders broke the power of the Seljuk Turks in Syria. Zangi, a Muslim noble from Mosul (now in northern Iraq), defeated a number of European crusaders and Seljuks, pushing them out of northern Syria. Zangi's son, Nureddin, succeeded his father and moved the capital of his growing kingdom first to Aleppo and then to Damascus.

SALADIN

As sultan (ruler) of Syria, Nureddin responded to an Egyptian leader's request for help both in settling an internal dispute and in stopping the crusaders. Nureddin sent one of his armies and his ablest general, Saladin, to the Egyptian royal court in 1169. Saladin became influential in the Egyptian administration and finally took control of Egypt in 1171. After Nureddin's death in 1174, Saladin became sultan of both Egypt and Syria.

After Saladin brought the independent armies of several Muslim nobles under his control, he used his newly unified forces to attack the crusaders. Saladin pushed the European armies out of Jerusalem in

1188. Muslim and Christian forces in other parts of the Middle East continued to fight until 1192. In that year, the two groups agreed to end the war. The agreement allowed Christians to have access to

Born in 1138, Saladin became the Islamic Empire's most successful commander. His battles against the Christian forces of England's Richard the Lion-hearted led to a truce in 1192. In addition to protecting Islamic territory, Saladin fostered education and funded public-works projects. His military successes gave Muslims pride in their faith and achievements.

Jerusalem in Palestine and to establish a limited number of outposts on Syria's coast.

Mongols, Mamluks, and Ottomans

After Saladin's death in 1192, Syria again broke into several states. In 1260 the Mongols, skilled warriors from central Asia, set upon Syria for the first time. Under their leader Hulegu Khan, the Mongols killed thousands of people and destroyed many mosques, homes, and aqueducts.

The Mongols attacked Syria several times in the thirteenth and fourteenth centuries. Forces from the Mamluk dynasty, which had established itself in Egypt in 1250, fought the Mongols in Syria during the 1300s and claimed the region as part of the Mamluk kingdom. Despite repeated Mongol raids, the Mamluks founded a prosperous realm. The most destructive Mongol attack came in 1402, when Timur the Lame (called Tamerlane in the West) captured and plundered Damascus.

Syria did not easily recover from the damage inflicted by Timur and his troops. The Mamluks continued to rule the area but became less effective. In 1516 the Ottoman Turks, founders of an Islamic empire in central Asia, defeated the Mamluks at Aleppo and started their 300-year rule of Syria. The Ottomans eventually controlled Anatolia, a section of southeastern Europe, most of southwestern Asia, and part of northern Africa.

The Ottomans ruled their empire through pashas—leaders who were given complete authority over their areas. The pashas employed local civic and religious officials to collect taxes, to establish courts, and to govern communities.

Under the pashas' leadership, Syria lost its economic vitality. Heavy taxes and

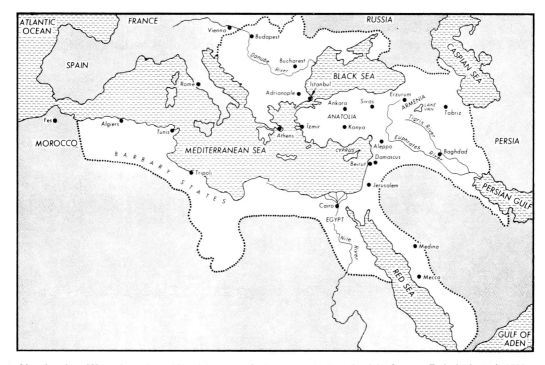

After decades of Mongol attacks and Mamluk control, Syria came under the rule of the Ottoman Turks in the early 1500s. Although the Ottomans established a stable government, heavy taxes weakened Syria economically. Also included in the Turkish empire were parts of Europe, North Africa, and other sections of the Middle East.

inefficient management hampered growth. Little trade occurred between Syria and other regions, which further reduced revenues. Damascus became a mere rest-stop for Muslims traveling from the north on their religious journey to the holy city of Mecca in Arabia. By the late 1700s, Syria's thriving economy and strong culture were things of the past.

European Intervention

As Syria slipped into a decline, events occurred in the Middle East that would affect Syria's future. In 1799 the French general Napoleon Bonaparte invaded Egypt to gain control of a trade route to India. For a brief period, he also occupied part of the Syrian coast.

The French attack illustrated the growing interest of European powers in the Middle East, especially as they saw the Ottoman Empire start to fall apart. Intent upon expanding their colonial holdings and trade routes, Europeans tried to establish power bases in the region. They saw Syria's commercial possibilities and hoped to gain control of the strategically located territory.

In the nineteenth century, France had ties with the Maronites—Christians in Greater Syria who were under the guidance of the Roman Catholic Church. The British developed a connection with the Druze, a religious group that had evolved from Islam in the eleventh century.

Hostilities broke out between the Druze and the Maronites in 1860. The Druze killed 10,000 Maronites, while losing few of their own fighters. French troops intervened, and the French government forced the Ottomans to establish Lebanon—a mostly Christian province, separate from Syria.

Many Syrians had grown restless with the inefficient and burdensome Ottoman government. The introduction of European forces and European ideas of independence—as well as the weakness of Ottoman rule—caused Syrians to begin considering self-government.

In response to Syria's concerns, Ottoman officials attempted reforms, but the changes met with limited success. Syrian taxes continued to be high, and the people objected when their young men were drafted into the Ottoman army. As the Syrians demanded relief, the Ottomans

In 1918, at the end of World War I, Arab forces entered Damascus after the defeat of the Ottoman army.

tried to suppress them. By the beginning of the twentieth century, an Arab independence movement had begun in Syria.

World Wars and the French Mandate

World War I (1914–1918) broke out just as the Arab movement toward self-rule was gaining momentum. During the conflict, members of Syrian nationalist groups participated in battles that pitted Britain, France, and Russia against Germany and Ottoman Turkey. The nationalists expected that an independent Syrian state would develop after the war.

British officials and Arab nobles wanted Hussein ibn Ali, the head of an influential Arab family, to encourage Arabs to fight against the Ottoman Turks. Led by his son Faisal, Hussein's forces launched their first attack in 1916. With the assistance of a British officer named T. E. Lawrence, Arab troops took Damascus in 1918, and Faisal became military governor.

After the war ended in 1918, Syrians organized a national congress that elected Faisal king of Syria, which at that time included Palestine and Transjordan (now Jordan). Faisal declared Arabic the country's official language and devoted much of the newly independent kingdom's resources to education. Syrian leaders also began to write a constitution. France and Britain, however, refused to recognize Syria as an independent nation.

DIVISION OF GREATER SYRIA

To maintain their power base in the Middle East, the French blocked Faisal's efforts to form a Syrian kingdom. Instead, France sought to establish a mandate (decree of legal control) over Syria. At a meeting in Europe, France and Britain—the primary victors in World War I—decided who would control the Arab territories taken from the Ottoman Turks. Both European nations believed that these regions might hold valuable oil reserves.

Photo by Bettmann Archive

Prince Faisal ibn Hussein was a leader in the Arab revolt against Ottoman rule in World War I. In 1918 a national congress named him king of Syria. During the postwar peace conferences, however, Britain and France claimed former Ottoman territories, including Syria, for themselves. European agreements rejected the newly independent kingdom and made Syria a French colony. In 1920 Faisal left the country and later became king of Iraq.

The basis for dividing the area was the Sykes-Picot Agreement, a document that representatives of the British and the French governments had signed secretly in 1916. According to this agreement, France would rule Syria and Lebanon, and Britain would have authority over Palestine, Transjordan, and Iraq. Ignoring Faisal's protests, the Europeans set up control of Arab lands according to the document's terms. The French mandate in Syria came into effect on July 15, 1920, and Faisal left the country.

The Europeans' decision to split Arab territory in this way led to anti-Western bitterness that still affects events in the Middle East. Arab nationalism grew, as did Pan-Arabism—a movement to establish a single Arab state in the region. The French divided Syria into several areas and administered them through a French high commissioner in Beirut, the capital of Lebanon. Hostilities continued to build in the next 25 years, however, as the French censored newspapers, imposed the French language in schools, and refused to set a timetable for eventual self-rule.

In 1925 Syrians who were bitter about the division of Greater Syria and about Western authority revolted against the French. Using great force, including bombardment, French troops put down the rebellion. Syrian dissatisfaction again mounted in 1939. In that year, France gave Turkey the northwestern district of Alexandretta, which Arab nationalists claimed. When World War II also broke out in 1939, Syrians were ready for change.

WORLD WAR II

The war again pitted France, Britain, and their allies against Germany. In 1940 France fell to Nazi German forces, and the French government came under Germany's authority. This change allowed the Germans to appoint the French person who would serve as high commissioner of Syria. In 1941 soldiers from Britain, Jordan, and Free France (France's anti-German resistance movement) overthrew the new colonial administration in Syria.

After the removal of the representatives of German power, Free French authorities ran Syria. The group's leader—General Charles de Gaulle—promised the territory eventual self-rule. By the time the war ended in 1945, France's allies—the Soviet Union, the United States, and Great Britain—had recognized the independent status of Syria. Nevertheless, France continued to control the colony, and French troops remained on Syrian soil.

Independence

After World War II, Syria was still technically under French authority. Nevertheless, Syria became a member of the United Nations (UN). De Gaulle, leader of the newly formed French government, resisted the Syrian drive for independence. France wanted to have special economic status in Syria and refused to pull out its army until Syria agreed to French terms.

In May 1945, Syrians protested in the streets of Damascus, Aleppo, Homs, and Hama against the French presence. Fighting erupted in the capital, and the French again bombed the city. Britain threatened to send its troops into Syria against France, and the UN pressured France to recognize Syria's independence. On April 17, 1946, the French finally evacuated their troops, and Syria became a fully self-governing republic.

Photo by UPI/Bettmann Newsphotos

Many Syrians resented the French presence, and in 1925 fighting broke out. The French bombarded the capital, destroying homes, offices, and ancient sites.

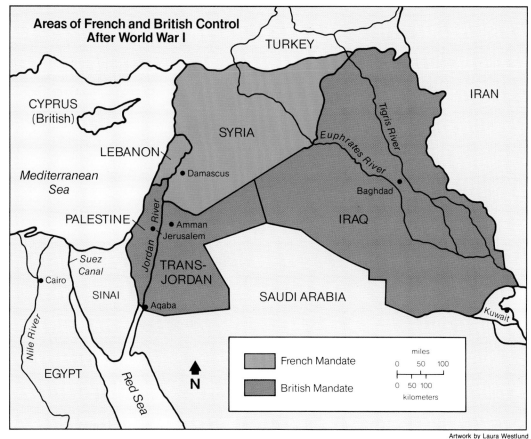

Areas of French and British Control After World War I

After World War I, Britain and France divided much of the Middle East into mandated territories, where the Europeans exercised authority. Strong opposition to France's control of Syria continued in the 1930s and 1940s, until Syria achieved its independence in 1946. The Europeans' division of the Middle East caused bitterness among peoples in the region, and tensions erupted into full-scale wars in later decades. Many of the conflicts were between Israel, created from a British mandate, and Syria.

The new country faced many problems, including a new political situation in the Middle East. Many Arabs refused to accept the establishment in 1948 of the Jewish State of Israel. It had been created from part of the British mandate territory of Palestine. That same year, Syria and other Arab countries attacked Israel in the hope of regaining what they regarded as Arab territory. Israel won the war, and Syrians blamed their own leaders for the defeat. After losing the war, Syria remained strongly opposed to a Jewish homeland in the Middle East.

Searching for Unity

The loss of the 1948 war to the Israelis merely added to the instability within Syria. The nation underwent three coups d'état (sudden overthrows of government) in 1949 alone. In that year, the military began to play a key role in Syrian political life. General Adib Shishakli led the third coup of 1949 and seized control of the government. By 1954 this military dictator had also been overthrown. The officers who ousted Shishakli allowed a group of civilian politicians to form an administration.

33

Gamal Abdel Nasser, the president of the newly formed United Arab Republic (UAR), addressed Syrian troops in Damascus in 1958. The UAR, made up of Syria and Egypt, lasted only until the early 1960s.

Photo by UPI/Bettmann Newsphotos

A new political organization, the Baath party, gained strength in the mid-1950s. Put together by Michel Aflaq, a Christian, and Salah Bitar, a Sunni Muslim, the Baath program focused on distributing land more evenly among the nation's people. The party also wanted to develop unity (Pan-Arabism) among the different Arab regions. Many of the group's members favored a socialist form of government. Shared ownership of industries and social equality were among their national goals. After Shishakli's fall, a number of Baathists won seats in the national legislature and began to lay the foundation for their eventual rule in Syria.

The hopes of many Syrians for a united Arab nation became a reality in 1958. The Pan-Arab movement had been gaining momentum for some time. Its most vocal supporter in the region was Egypt's president Gamal Abdel Nasser. Syrians turned to Nasser to lead a combined Syrian-Egyptian state known as the United Arab Republic (UAR).

Many Syrians, however, were disappointed when the new nation located its central administration in the Egyptian part of the country. In addition, a large number of Egyptians gained high posts in the Syrian sector of the UAR. Egypt had a larger population, a more developed economy, and a dynamic leader in Nasser. As a result, the Syrians felt that the distribution of power between the two parts of the UAR was uneven.

The Arab union lasted only until 1961. At that time, Syrian army officers seized control of their territory and withdrew from the UAR. The leaders of the revolt were primarily from the Alawi religious group—a minority Islamic sect. They rejected the leadership of Aflaq and Bitar and developed their own branch of the Baath party. Less committed to Arab unity than their predecessors, these officers focused their attention on the economic development of Syria.

The Baath Party and Hafiz al-Assad

Several factions of the Baath party struggled for control of the country in the 1960s. Even within the military wing of the party, divisions split the membership. Ten coups occurred between 1963 and 1970, and unlike most of the previous overthrows, some of these changes were violent. Slowly, General Hafiz al-Assad—an Alawi—and his followers began to gather strength in the Baath ranks. Those Baathists who had been overthrown left the country and lived in exile. Iraq gave refuge to some of the fleeing Baathists, and this action created tension between Syria and Iraq.

The continuing Arab conflict with Israel also helped Baath members and General Assad to gather support within Syria. In June 1967, Israel clashed with Egypt, Jordan, and Syria in a war that lasted six days. The Israelis gained a significant amount of Arab territory, including Syria's Golan Heights. The loss of this area created more disunity in Syrian politics, as leaders blamed one another for the defeat.

Assad took advantage of the confusion to increase his political power in the region. He supported Palestinian refugees who had fled areas held by Israel and had settled in Jordan. Assad also backed Palestinian efforts to form political forces —among them, the Palestine Liberation Organization (PLO). In 1970, to prevent civil war, King Hussein of Jordan ordered his army to push the PLO and other Palestinian groups into Syria and Lebanon.

Assad funded these Palestinian groups, who used terrorist tactics against the Israelis. Palestinian militias in Syria, however, had to submit to close supervision from Assad's military forces. Eventually, almost all Palestinians moved into Lebanon, where they could receive weapons and money from Syria without directly being under Syrian control.

ASSAD TAKES POWER

As these external changes occurred, Assad made his move to take over Syria. In October 1970, his troops surrounded a meeting of Baath party leaders. Because of this show of force, Assad was able to take control of the party. In 1971 he became president of Syria, running as the only candidate in a national election.

Assad's new government took the holdings of many wealthy landowners and redistributed the acreages in smaller plots to farm workers. Assad strengthened his power by naming many of his fellow Alawis to high positions in the Baath party and the Syrian government. These moves put him in conflict with the majority religious population—the Sunni Muslims—who did not like Assad's strict control. The president's security forces exercised harsh measures— including arrest, torture, and execution— against Assad's opponents.

Two years after Assad came to power, Egypt and Syria joined in a surprise attack against Israel. In this 1973 war, the Syrian forces at first regained part of the Golan Heights lost in 1967. But eventually the Israelis overran the Syrian troops and occupied even more ground. Only through

Photo by UPI/Bettmann Newsphotos

Wars between Arab states and Israel broke out in the 1960s and 1970s. In 1973, when Syria and Egypt attacked Israel, the Syrian army made some initial gains. Later, however, Israeli troops reoccupied land called the Golan Heights. Here, Syrian soldiers climb Mount Hermon—which lies north of the Golan Heights—to engage Israeli fighters.

Syria flies the flag designed for the UAR as its national emblem even though the UAR broke up in 1961. Red, white, and black are the traditional colors of the Pan-Arab movement for unity among Arab countries. Green – used in the two stars – is the color of Islam.

negotiations at the end of the war did Syria finally get back a small part of the Golan Heights. Compared to other military encounters with Israel, Syrians considered the 1973 war a victory. They remain opposed to all Arab-Israeli peace efforts in the region.

Recent Events

Following the 1973 war, Syria turned its attention from Israel to one of its other neighbors—Lebanon. Because Syrians traditionally consider Lebanon an extended part of their nation, Assad and his army have often intervened in Lebanon's internal affairs. At various times, Syria has backed several different—even opposing—Lebanese groups to promote its own interests in the region.

Several Islamic factions supported by Syria entered the Lebanese civil war, which the nation's Christians and Muslims began fighting in the mid-1970s. In 1976 a Lebanese Christian faction asked Syria for help in stopping the conflict. In response, Assad eventually sent as many as 40,000 troops to prevent the break-up of Lebanon. The move also served his own interests by keeping the Lebanese-Syrian border stable. But the Syrian military presence did not halt the violence in Lebanon and in some cases increased it. The Syrian army also took control of portions of eastern and northern Lebanon.

By the end of the 1980s, many Lebanese—especially Christians—were trying to push the Syrians out of the country. Assad and the Islamic militias he supports responded by raising the intensity of the

Syrian soldiers guard a battle-scarred street in Beirut, the capital of Lebanon. Since 1976, when Lebanon's civil war reached a peak, Syrian troops have controlled parts of Beirut and the Lebanese countryside. Syria also supports Muslim factions fighting in Lebanon.

fighting against Christian factions. Representatives of the UN and the Arab League (an organization that promotes Arab unity) continue to promote a cease-fire in the region. It remains to be seen, however, if Syria will let go of its power over Lebanon's future for the sake of peace.

EAST-WEST TENSIONS

With its new involvement in Lebanon, the Syrian government decided to increase Syria's military strength by obtaining more weapons. Throughout the 1980s, a supply of surface-to-air missiles arrived from the Soviet Union. Syria had been getting small-scale arms from the Soviet Union since 1956, and in 1989 about 6,000 Soviet military advisers were living in Syria.

Many Western nations, including the United States and Great Britain, charge Syria with supporting the terrorist activities of Palestinian groups. These claims are difficult to prove, but evidence links Syria to terrorist bombings in Europe in 1985 and 1986. Syrian officials deny any connection with these events. They also refuse to take responsibility for the actions of any Palestinian groups, even of those that began operating from Syria in the 1980s. Many representatives of Western countries insist that Syria influences some of the Muslim factions in Lebanon that hold Western hostages.

The Soviet Union has fostered a relationship with Syria since the 1950s. In 1974 Syrian president Hafiz al-Assad (seated left) watched as Soviet leader Leonid Brezhnev (right) signed an accord. The document provided for economic and technical cooperation between the two countries.

37

Although weakened by a heart attack in 1983, Assad is firmly in control of Syria's affairs. A stubborn force in the Arab League (a group that fosters Arab unity), Assad has sometimes made decisions that have isolated Syria from neighboring Arab states.

CONFLICT WITH IRAQ

Relations with Iraq, Syria's eastern neighbor, worsened in the 1980s. A Baath party leader runs each country, but some issues divide the two nations. For example, they dispute each other's water rights to the Euphrates River. They also disagree over the operation of an oil pipeline (closed since 1982) that connects Kirkuk in Iraq to the Syrian port of Baniyas. Syria has accused Iraq of conspiring to overthrow Syria's government by assassinating high-ranking officials. Iraq has made the same claims against Syria.

As a result of these tensions, Syria sided with Iran during the Iran-Iraq war. This stance put Syria at odds with most Arab states of the Middle East, which supported Iraq. Some Arab nations decreased their financial aid to Syria because of the conflict. A UN-sponsored cease-fire in August 1988 stopped the war and gave Syria an opportunity to improve its relations with other Arab countries. The cease-fire did not solve Syria's feud with Iraq, which began to supply weapons to the Lebanese Christian groups that are fighting Syria's militias in Lebanon.

INTERNAL PROBLEMS

In addition to facing difficulties with neighboring nations, Assad also confronts challenges to his leadership from within the country. The Muslim Brotherhood, a Sunni group that wants Syria to be governed according to Islamic principles, has held demonstrations in several Syrian cities. The group has also bombed buildings that house Baath headquarters and has assassinated Alawi leaders who are close to Assad.

In 1982 government troops responded with great force to an uprising that the Muslim Brotherhood started in Hama. The Syrian army crushed the rebel soldiers in two weeks of fighting, killing more than 10,000 of the brotherhood's members. Artillery fire leveled the old section of the city. The defeat considerably weakened the Muslim Brotherhood, which has joined with other groups that oppose Assad to establish the National Alliance for the Liberation of Syria.

Assad also faces the problem of Syria's unstable economic outlook. Plagued by frequent droughts, falling export income, and decreased funds from other Arab states, the nation's economy has steadily declined. In addition, after Assad suffered a heart attack in 1983, his health became a serious concern. Rivals to his authority have begun positioning themselves to take power. Although Assad's hold on the reins of government is strong, the lack of an agreed-upon successor causes uncertainty about the future.

Government

The constitution of Syria, written in 1973, establishes the nation as a socialist state in which the government controls the economy. Citizens over 18 elect a president who must be a Muslim and who is nominated by the Baath party—the nation's official political organization. The president, who serves a seven-year term, has wide powers, which include naming a cabinet, commanding the army, and dissolving the legislature.

Syria's legislature, or people's council, has 195 members. Elected to terms of four years, legislators meet three times each year to debate government policy and to enact laws. Some members must be from a group that the constitution describes as "workers and peasants." This provision attempts to ensure widespread representation of the Syrian population.

A high judicial council, of which the nation's president is the head, appoints judges to Syria's courts. The top judicial level is the court of cassation, which hears final appeals from lower courts. The mid-range judiciary is made up of provincial courts of appeal. On the local level are courts of first instance, which handle minor offenses. Islamic religious courts interpret *sharia*—Islamic law—in cases involving family matters.

Syria is divided into 14 provinces, one of which is Damascus. The national government appoints a governor for each province who is then assisted by a provincial council. A number of officials from the central government join each local council to help administer the province and to maintain a strong link with the capital.

Courtesy of Syrian Ministry of Tourism

The Syrian Parliament holds its legislative sessions in this cream-colored building topped by the Syrian hawk—a symbol found on the country's coat of arms.

A market in Aleppo, where food and other goods are for sale, reflects the growth of Syria's urban areas.

3) The People

More than 12 million people live in Syria, which is growing rapidly in population. Its present rate of increase—3.8 percent—suggests that the number of Syrians could double in 18 years. Another indication of the nation's growth—as well as of improved health conditions—is the large proportion of young Syrians. Nearly 50 percent of the population are under the age of 15.

A long-standing problem for Syria is the disunity among its citizens. People tend to identify strongly with a religious sect or an ethnic community, and historically these groups have opposed one another. Thus, at a given time, being a Kurd or a Druze may overshadow being a Syrian. The strength of these specific loyalties has hampered national unity throughout the twentieth century.

Arabs relax beneath woven tapestries and ornamental plates in a rural home.

Ethnic Groups

Most Syrians share an Arab heritage and speak Arabic, the nation's official language. Although Arabs dwell throughout the country, about half live in cities, where they often speak French in addition to Arabic. Most of the remaining Arab population are farmers and shepherds in the mountains and plains. Bedouin, who form a small percentage of Syria's Arabs, make their homes, at least for part of the year, in the desert.

Many urban Arabs participate in both traditional and modern lifestyles. Syrian cities usually are centered around an old commercial and residential section, which may predate the Greek era. Various *suqs* (markets) display crafts, foods, and other goods in a traditional way. Beyond the old city, however, are modern buildings, including businesses and homes that use the up-to-date technology found in urban areas worldwide. The Syrian government and local industries are the largest employers of city-dwelling Arabs, and Arab women have a prominent place in the urban work force.

In contrast, rural Arabs continue to follow a lifestyle that has changed little in the twentieth century. The main livelihood is still farming, although more people now own the land they work than in previous decades. Following their traditional roles, most rural Arab men farm, and most women raise children and have some farming duties. Because of recent improvements in transportation, villagers can travel to

Bedouin children chat amid the ruins of Palmyra. The girl on the right wears a *kaffiyeh,* or checkered cloth, as a head covering.

41

The usual dwelling for desert Bedouin is a dark, camel-hair tent. The entire family lives beneath this woven shelter until it is unstaked and folded up to prepare for the next move.

Courtesy of Bill Hendricks

cities for medical care and their children may attend classes in larger towns. Some young rural people also go to urban areas in search of jobs.

Most of the Bedouin are nomads, herding their livestock through the Syrian Desert on a seasonal search for water and food. They share this nomadic lifestyle with Bedouin who migrate between Iraq, Saudi Arabia, Kuwait, and Jordan. Some members of this group have sought a more settled lifestyle in recent years.

Highly regarded by other Arabs because of their reputation for courage and loyalty, traditional Bedouin live in large, woven tents. Each tent represents a family, and a group of families makes up a clan. Bedouin form strong family ties and are known for their hospitality in the desert's difficult environment.

NON-ARAB MINORITIES

About 10 percent of the total Syrian population belong to non-Arab ethnic groups—mainly to Kurdish, Armenian, and Turkoman communities. The Kurds, who make up 6 percent, inhabit the northeastern corner of Syria, near Iraq and Turkey. A Sunni Islamic people, the Kurds have preserved their distinct culture by living in remote areas. The Syrian Kurds are only a small part of the Middle East's Kurdish population. Several million more inhabit the region where Iraq, Turkey, and Syria meet.

Ancestors of Syria's Armenians fled Turkey in the early twentieth century to escape Turkish oppression. Forming about 3 percent of Syria's total population, they live mainly in and around Aleppo. A Christian group, the Armenians continue to follow their own traditions and to run their own schools. Most Armenians reside in cities and are often traders or artisans.

Syria's small population of Turkomans originated in central Asia. Once a nomadic people, the group now herds livestock in Al-Jazira and farms small plots near Aleppo. Although they speak Turkic, many Turkomans also use Arabic. In addition, Turkomans are Sunni Muslims and share religious beliefs with Syria's Arab Sunnis.

Religion

Religious ties also play an important part in Syrian society. In fact, the people tend to give stronger loyalty to an ethnic or religious group than to the nation.

ISLAM

About 85 percent of Syria's population follow the Islamic faith. Begun in the seventh century by the prophet Muhammad, Islam has two main sects—the Sunnis and the Shiites. They both support the central practices of the faith. In Syria, as in most of the Arab world, the Sunnis are the largest group, making up about 72 percent of the nation's Islamic population. Sunnis dominated political activity for decades, until the Assad regime took power. The number of Shiites in Syria is small.

Both Sunni and Shiite Muslims are encouraged to fulfill certain religious duties. Believers pray to Allah (the Arabic word for God) five times daily facing in the direction of Mecca, Saudi Arabia, where Muhammad was born. They are called to prayer by muezzins (criers), who chant from minarets (towers). Muslims fast from sunrise to sunset during the holy month of Ramadan and are encouraged to give donations to the poor. Male Muslims try to make a pilgrimage to Mecca once in their lifetime.

In addition to Sunnis and Shiites, the Islamic population in Syria includes two smaller sects. The nation's largest religious minority is the Alawis, who form about 10 percent of the Islamic group. Their beliefs include practices from Syria's Christian and Islamic periods. Alawis celebrate Christmas and Easter, for example, and also recognize traditional Islamic duties. Long persecuted for their religious ideas, the Alawis gained great power in 1971, when one of them—Hafiz al-Assad—became Syria's president.

Smaller in number than the Alawis are the Ismailis. Members of this group are closely related to Shiites and sometimes are called Seveners. The name comes from a split among Shiites that took place in

His head wrapped in a kaffiyeh, a Syrian Muslim reads the Koran (sacred Islamic writings) in the Umayyad Mosque in Damascus. Faithful Muslims pray five times a day and fulfill other Islamic obligations as well. About 85 percent of Syria's population follow the religion of Islam.

Photo by Drs. A. A. M. van der Heyden, Naarden, the Netherlands

43

about the ninth century. Until that time, all Shiites accepted the same succession of six imams—holy men with spiritual and earthly authority. A disagreement arose among Shiites about Ismail, the seventh imam of Islam. One group, the Ismailis, came to recognize no imams after Ismail. Most other Shiites supported a total of 12 imams, and members of this group are sometimes referred to as Twelvers.

MINORITY RELIGIONS

Christians, who account for about 10 percent of the Syrian religious population, belong to many sects. The largest Christian groups are Greek Orthodox, Armenian Orthodox, Syrian Orthodox, and Greek Catholic. Other Christians include Maronites, Nestorians, Chaldeans, Roman Catholics, and Protestants.

The Druze in Syria make up about 3 percent of the religious population and live mostly in the southwestern district of Jabal al-Arab. They are a tightly knit, fiercely independent, and secretive group. Originating as a branch of Shiite Islam in the eleventh century, the Druze do not consider themselves part of the Muslim population. They derive their name from a mystic named Ismail al-Darazi. Al-Darazi was a follower of Al-Hakim, whom the Druze believe was an earthly presence of God.

Language and Literature

Nearly all Syrians speak Arabic, the nation's official language and the main tongue of the entire Arab world. Scholars note three stages in the development of Arabic. The Koran, Islam's ancient book of sacred writings, is written in classical Arabic, which was spoken in the seventh century. Almost any educated Arabic-

Photo by The Hutchison Library

Turbanned *ulema,* or Islamic scholars, carry their shoes as they enter the Umayyad Mosque. Facilities in the mosque's courtyard allow believers to wash before entering the holy place.

Photo by The Hutchison Library

This Druze elder is part of a secretive religious sect that is centered in southwestern Syria.

Read from right to left, Arabic letters can be written in different styles. Thickly drawn characters *(top row)* are for everyday use, while a more flowing form *(middle row)* is used for special occasions. The most ornate lettering *(bottom row)* appears primarily in headlines and titles. Although many dialects of spoken Arabic exist, the alphabet used to write the language is the same throughout the Arab world.

speaker can understand modern standard Arabic, a later literary language. Within Syria, a separate dialect called Syrian Arabic is used in daily speech and varies in pronunciation.

Kurdish is spoken in the extreme north-eastern corner of the country, where the nation's Kurds reside. Unlike Arabic, which is part of the Semitic family of languages, Kurdish has its roots in Indo-Iranian languages. The Armenian community uses Armenian at home, and the Turkomans usually communicate with their own Turkic language. Because of colonial influences earlier in the twentieth century, many educated people in large cities speak French as a second language.

Like other Middle Eastern countries, Syria takes great pride in its long tradition of oral and written poetry. Among the nation's most famous poets is Al-Mutanabbi, a tenth-century writer who traveled to Iraq and Egypt. Al-Maarri—a teacher and philosopher—wrote verse and sermons in the eleventh century.

The works of these intellectuals developed beside a tradition of oral legends. Storytellers entertained their listeners with tales of ancient heroes and heroines. Many of these imaginative stories became the basis of *The Thousand and One Nights* —a collection of age-old Arab folktales compiled in the 1500s.

Modern poets include Mohammad Maghout, Fayez Khaddour, and Mamdou Adwan. Their writings reflect the post-independence struggles that Syria has faced. Many Syrian authors whose works

Courtesy of Library of Congress

In a fanciful drawing, an Arab storyteller captivates the patrons of a coffeehouse in Damascus. A centuries-old form of entertainment, storytelling survives in present-day Syria. Some of the most famous tales became part of *The Thousand and One Nights,* which features the adventures of Aladdin and Ali Baba.

have not been approved by the Assad regime publish outside Syria, mainly in Lebanon.

Education and Health

Since independence in 1946, the Syrian government has tried to teach more citizens to read and write. About 47 percent of the population are literate. Schools encourage young Syrians to acquire skills needed in industry and modern agriculture. The administration also sees education as a primary way of training young citizens in the ideas of the Baath party. Fewer girls attend school than boys, and overall literacy figures tend to be lower for women than they are for men.

Schooling is compulsory for children between 6 and 11 years of age, and most

Students at a primary school in northern Syria participate in a reading lesson. Most young Syrians attend school at the elementary level.

A teacher unravels the complexities of electronics to a group of interested students. Technical training is an expanding part of Syria's post-secondary school system.

A Syrian doctor examines her patient at a clinic that offers general medical services. As a result of better facilities, the number of young and old Syrians is growing. In 1990, 49 percent were under the age of 15, and 4 percent were over 65.

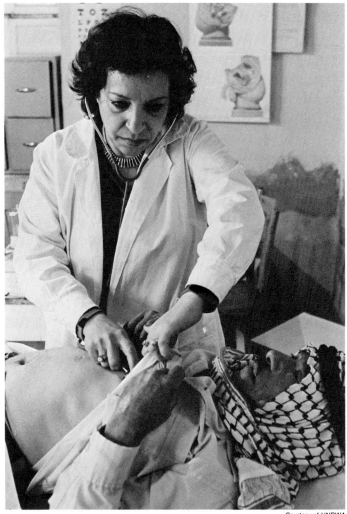

Courtesy of UNRWA

Syrian boys and girls attend elementary classes. At the secondary level, however, fewer young Syrians follow the six-year course. Students have access to higher education at several universities and technical-training institutes. The University of Damascus was founded in 1923, and the University of Aleppo opened in 1960. The total enrollment at these and other post-secondary schools is over 60,000.

Syria's dramatic population increase since independence is partially due to improvements in health care, which is generally provided at no cost to the patient. As a result of better medical services, fewer babies die, and adults live longer. Although hospitals and medical personnel tend to cluster in urban areas—especially in Damascus and Aleppo—clinics have opened throughout the country.

A national program of vaccinations has controlled some illnesses—such as malaria and tuberculosis. Cases of diphtheria and trachoma (an eye disease), however, are still widely reported in rural areas. Despite these remaining difficulties, Syria's infant mortality rate of 48 deaths in every 1,000 live births is low for western Asia. Life expectancy, which was 65 years in 1989, is average for the region.

47

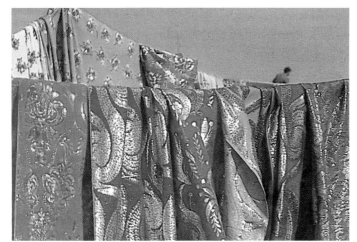

Large samples of silk brocade hang from sturdy ropes. The silver and gold threads that are woven into the fabric create an ornate, shimmering effect in the cloth.

The Arts

As a crossroads of trade, Syria has welcomed artists and artistic forms from Africa, Asia, and Europe. Many of the traditional styles of Syrian crafts reflect these varied influences.

Fine, handmade brocade—silk fabric richly interwoven with silver and gold threads—continues to be made in Damascus and Homs. Artisans use an ancient process—named damascene, after Damascus—to inlay precious stones on trays

Glassblowers fashion glass objects by gathering a glob of molten glass on the end of their hollow blowpipe. By blowing gently into the tube and by twirling it, the molten substance can be stretched into the desired shape.

48

Made of wood, metal, stone, and glass, a door of the Umayyad Mosque has an ornate, geometric pattern. The process of inlaying cut pieces of glass or stone into an outlined form is called damascene, after the capital city of Damascus.

Courtesy of Syrian Ministry of Tourism

The front of the Umayyad Mosque is decorated with a floral design. Islam forbids the use of human and animal figures in religious decoration. As a result, most mosques contain complex, but non-figurative, art.

and plaques. Bazaars often display finely crafted pieces of ebony, lemonwood, and rosewood. Glassblowing is also an ancient art, and modern practitioners make hand-blown jugs, vases, and glassware.

Because the Koran forbids the use of human figures in Islamic decoration, Arab artistic output in Syria has focused on geometric and floral patterns. The mosaic tile work of mosques and the ornately written pages from the Koran present a variety of beautiful styles and shapes. Calligraphy—the art of hand-lettering—has enjoyed a revival in Syria in recent years.

Reading poetry aloud is still a popular form of entertainment in Syria, and Syrian musicians often accompany modern readers. Traditional instruments from the region include the *oud* (an Arabian lute), the *rebab* (a fiddle), and the *kanoon* (a zither). Musicians also play Syrian folk music at local and regional celebrations.

Photo by The Hutchison Library

Syrian copper workers gather in a Damascus street to practice their craft. By hammering the metal, the artisans shape trays and containers.

Food and Recreation

Syrian cuisine resembles the cooking of other Middle Eastern countries, with many dishes based on lamb, eggplant, rice, chick-peas, yogurt, and *bulgur* (cracked wheat). Other meat, fresh vegetables, and seasonal or dried fruits occasionally supplement the usual foods.

Traditional meals include *hummos,* a finely blended mixture of chick-peas, lemon juice, garlic, and ground sesame seeds. Flat rounds of bread usually accompany hummos, which is eaten by dipping bread in the thick sauce. Tabbouleh combines bulgur with tomatoes, parsley, onions, oil, and lemon juice. Main dishes often use lamb as the basic meat, although chicken is also popular. Most dinners end with sweet Turkish coffee or strong tea served in small glasses. City dwellers have a more varied diet, with greater amounts of meat and fish, than rural people do.

Syrians, especially in urban areas, enjoy a variety of recreational activities. Movie

Cooks make *hummos* by blending chick-peas, lemon juice, garlic, and ground sesame seeds into a paste. This thick spread, sometimes garnished with parsley sprigs, is served with flat rounds of bread.

Near Aleppo, a vendor sells specially brewed coffee to passersby. The word *coffee* comes from the Arabic term *qahwa.* As served in Syria, the beverage is thick and sweet.

theaters are scattered throughout city neighborhoods. In Damascus, Syrians who enjoy Western entertainment go to nightclubs and discotheques.

Soccer, called football in Syria, is perhaps the nation's most popular sport. Basketball, tennis, boxing, and swimming also attract many enthusiasts. Young and old alike play chess, an ancient board game that may have originated in the Middle East. In recent years, Syrian women have become involved in sports, participating in national and international competitions held in the capital.

Young Syrians *(left)* play an informal game of basketball in a schoolyard. Older athletes who are members of a Syrian military unit *(below)* hoist their unit's insignia in the opening ceremonies of a national competition.

A herder grazes his sheep on grasses outside a fertilizer factory in Homs.

4) The Economy

Since the Baath party came to power, the government has directed Syria's economy. Socialist policies—such as shared land-ownership and state control of industries—dominate economic activities in the country.

The nation's financial status, however, has spiraled downward since the mid-1980s. At that time, oil profits, which provided the majority of Syria's earned foreign income, fell as world petroleum prices decreased. The country's Arab financial aid also declined because Syria backed Iran in its war against Iraq, which most other Arab states supported. The Syrian government cut some expenses and reduced imports to make up for its drop in income, but the regime continued to spend 50 percent of its budget on defense.

In the late 1980s, these difficulties put Syria's economy in an uncertain position. One hopeful sign is that Arab aid is again available now that Iran and Iraq are at peace. Oil production has increased recently, and agricultural development has improved crop yields.

The Petroleum Industry

Syria first awarded rights for oil exploration to a foreign firm in the 1930s. Until the 1960s, Western businesses dominated the nation's petroleum industry. Transferred from private to state control in 1964, the oil sector has only recently emerged as a big national money earner. The main fields lie at Qaratshuk, Suwaydiya, and Rumaylan in northeastern Syria. In the

1970s, foreign firms again acquired permits to explore for oil and found fields near Dayr al-Zawr in eastern Syria. An internal pipeline brings Syria's crude oil to refineries in the western part of the country.

Despite these finds, Syria's oil reserves are small compared to those of other Arab states in the region. The nation is estimated to pump about 200,000 barrels of petroleum per day. (Saudi Arabia produces about six million barrels daily.) Oil sales accounted for about half of the country's overall export income throughout the 1980s and became Syria's chief source of foreign revenue.

Along with crude oil exports, Syria once earned substantial income from transit fees for oil pipelines that cross the nation. Tapline—the Trans-Arabian Pipeline—linked Saudi Arabia's oil fields with the Lebanese port of Sidon. A section of the pipeline goes through Syria, but, because of conflicts in Lebanon, parts of Tapline have been closed. Another connection brought Iraq's crude oil from Kirkuk to a refinery at Homs. From there, an offshoot

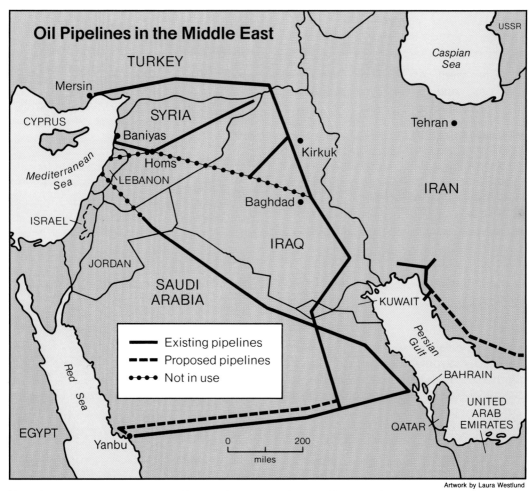

Artwork by Laura Westlund

Throughout the 1980s, when a war raged between Iraq and Iran, Syria used its oil pipelines as a political tool. For example, the Syrian government, which favored Iran in the fight, closed the pipeline from Iraq to Homs. The Lebanon-Saudi Arabia line also passed through Syria, but the link was shut down because of the Lebanese civil war. As a result of this closure, Syria lost substantial funds that it had been earning from transit fees.

Irrigation is needed to cultivate vegetables in this field near Aleppo. Most areas of Syria do not receive enough rain for farming without additional watering.

pipeline went to the port of Tripoli, Lebanon, and another led to Baniyas, Syria, on the Mediterranean. The outbreak of war between Iran and Iraq caused Syria to close this pipeline in 1982.

Since then, Iran has supplied Syria with low-cost or free crude oil, which Syria refines at its plants in Homs and Baniyas. To further involve itself in the oil industry, Syria joined the Organization of Petroleum Exporting Countries (OPEC) in 1976. This group sets quotas and prices for oil in world markets.

Agriculture

In the 1980s, the Syrian government took steps to revitalize the farming sector. Once the mainstay of the nation's economy, agriculture has dropped to second place—behind oil—as a foreign-income earner. The number of people involved in farming has also fallen. Fifty percent of the population farmed in the 1970s, but only 30 percent worked in agriculture in the 1980s. The drop occurred when many Syrians sought jobs in cities or in the oil sector. Formerly self-sufficient in food production, Syria has been importing cereal grains and other foodstuffs in the last decade.

The contents of a market stall reflect the variety of crops that the country's farmers are able to grow.

55

With donkeys strapped to a plow, a farmer turns the earth in his field. Although modern agricultural equipment is used in some parts of Syria, small-scale farmers still employ traditional methods.

International agencies are helping Syria to produce more out-of-season food. These laborers are boxing a crop of Syrian-grown greenhouse cucumbers, which normally would have to be imported in winter.

Lack of water is the chief cause of agricultural decline. Rainfall enables only coastal farmers to grow crops. Farther inland, irrigation is essential for farming. The Euphrates and the Orontes rivers provide most of the water for irrigation. Opened in 1978, the Euphrates Dam was meant to double the amount of cropland. Low water levels and high costs have caused some operational problems. By late 1989, the project had increased farmable acreages by only 10 percent.

About 30 percent of Syria's land is farmed, primarily along the coast and in the north. Most farmers own their land, but other aspects of agriculture—such as marketing and transporting the goods—are in the government's hands. Although mechanization is becoming more common, many farmers still use traditional methods.

Cereal grains, cotton, sugar beets, tobacco, fruits, and vegetables are Syria's principal crops. The chief cereals are wheat and barley, with sorghum, millet, and corn in distant rankings. An age-old crop, cotton was once Syria's biggest export. The nation's textile mills use most of the cotton, but about 20 percent is still exported. Among orchard crops, olives are of first importance, and in the Aleppo area, pistachio nuts are grown. On the coastal plain and in northwestern Syria, farmers harvest grapes, which supply a small wine industry.

Sheep, poultry, and cattle are the leading livestock animals, with herds of both beef and dairy cattle increasing rapidly. The Bedouin raise most of the sheep in eastern Syria. When recent droughts decreased available scrub vegetation, some Bedouin brought their herds westward to farming areas. By the mid-1980s, Syria produced substantial amounts of meat and eggs but still imported milk products.

Among Syria's major orchard crops are nuts from pistachio trees. A young vendor weighs some ready-to-eat pistachios in his family's food stall.

Photo by Christine Osborne

Riding a donkey, a Bedouin herder watches over his flock.

Mining and Industry

Although oil is Syria's chief mineral, natural gas and phosphates also contribute to the mining sector's income. Of the nation's remaining deposits, only iron ore, asphalt, and salt exist in quantities large enough to earn money.

While searching for petroleum deposits in the northeastern part of the country, geologists discovered natural gas. The government allowed foreign firms to develop this resource, and groups from France, Czechoslovakia, and the United States built processing centers. The main refinery is at Homs, and another plant is under construction at Rumaylan.

Syria also contains large deposits of phosphate, which workers have extracted since the 1970s. The largest mine, located in central Syria, produces about one million tons of phosphate per year. Most of the output goes to Eastern European countries, while Syrian farmers use some of the phosphate as fertilizer.

Until the 1960s, Syria's industrial sector chiefly processed the country's agricul-

With the aid of tractors, workers mine phosphate in the Syrian Desert. Phosphates, used in making fertilizer and detergent, are an important Syrian export.

Wearing white veils, these Druze women weave a fine piece of cloth by hand. Textile production is also practiced on an industrial scale in the nation's large cities.

Crammed with bags of freshly picked cotton, a truck makes its way to a factory where the goods will be spun into yarn for cloth making.

tural products. Factory workers were employed mainly in making cigarettes, weaving cloth, extracting olive oil, and packing dried fruit. Although these industries are still important, the Syrian economy is no longer as dependent on them. New factories are now turning out glass, paper, fertilizers, cement, iron and steel, television sets, and household appliances.

Syria's textile industry remains a key part of the manufacturing sector. Locally grown cotton is spun into thread at factories in Aleppo, Hama, and Damascus. Workers weave cotton, wool, and other fabrics using modern techniques. A valued export since ancient times, silk brocade is still made by hand.

Transportation and Energy

As a major crossroads of trade, Syria has long had transportation networks for moving goods to international markets. These systems have historically been centered in western Syria. Since independence, the

59

Located near Damascus, this bridge is part of a motorway that leads from the capital to northern urban centers.

government has made an effort to extend roads and railways throughout the country. Yet, most Syrians do not own cars, and personal travel is often accomplished by bus, by train, or on foot.

Most of Syria's highways are in the west and cover about 5,000 miles of the country's territory. They run between Damascus and Syria's other large cities and carry about 95 percent of the nation's freight and passengers. Two-lane roads connect western towns and small settlements in northern and central Syria.

Two types of railways exist in Syria, both of which were originally built in the early 1900s. A narrow-gauge track was part of the Hejaz Railway that connected Damascus and Dara in Syria with cities in Lebanon and Jordan. In the 1980s, this railway covered about 200 miles of Syrian territory. Wider, standard-gauge track has been substantially expanded since independence. Rail connections are available for freight and passengers between major urban areas in western Syria. Track also crosses the width of the nation, linking Aleppo, Al-Raqqa, Dayr al-Zawr, Al-Hasaka, and Al-Qamishli.

As well as owning the railways, the Syrian government operates the national airline, Syrian Arab Airlines. It flies to many points in Asia, Europe, and Africa and maintains an international airport at Damascus. Smaller airfields exist at Aleppo, Latakia, Al-Qamishli, and Dayr al-Zawr. Syria's chief port facilities lie at Latakia, Tartus, and Baniyas. The opening of an oil refinery at Baniyas further increased the number of ships that arrived at its docks.

At one time, hydropower from the Euphrates and other dams fueled Syria's energy needs. The dams have been unable to meet increasing energy demands, however, and Syria has turned to alternate sources. Among these replacements are thermal plants, solar power, and nuclear reactors.

Even the use of these other sources has not prevented power outages in Syrian cities that can last up to four hours per day. In addition, industry—the main user of energy—has decreased production to accommodate frequent shortages of power. As a result, Syria's energy crunch has seriously affected manufacturing.

Photo by Christine Osborne

A freighter unloads its cargo at the port of Tartus in western Syria. Much of the country's international trade arrives by sea, mainly at Latakia, Tartus, and Baniyas.

Courtesy of Syrian Ministry of Tourism

Soviet loans and technology helped Syria to build the Euphrates Dam. When completed in the 1970s, it had the potential to meet 80 percent of Syria's electricity needs. But low water levels cause the dam's turbines often to operate below capacity, so that less energy is produced.

Photo by The Hutchison Library

Syria's main trade item is refined oil, which comes from facilities in Homs *(above)* and Baniyas.

Trade and Tourism

Throughout the 1980s, Syria spent more money on imports than it earned from the sale of its exports. As a result, the nation owed more than $400 million to foreign creditors in 1989. This negative economic situation has encouraged the government to improve its ability to grow food and to refine oil. In addition, Syria has recently shifted away from doing most of its business with Western industrialized countries. Once dependent on European sales and goods, Syria has turned increasingly to Eastern European nations and to other Arab states as customers and suppliers.

Syria's principal exports are oil, cotton, textiles, tobacco, phosphates, fruits, and vegetables. Communist nations buy 40 percent of Syria's exports, the European Community (EC) purchases about 30 per-

cent, and Asian and other Arab states order most of the remainder. Imports consist mainly of foodstuffs, fuels, machinery, vehicles, and other manufactured goods. Asian and Arab states furnish more than 30 percent of these products, the EC is the source of about 25 percent, and Communist countries provide roughly 10 percent.

The uncertain political situation in the Middle East has hampered the development of tourism in Syria. Nevertheless, the nation improved its facilities to make its archaeological treasures more accessible to foreigners. Nearly one million visitors came to Syria annually in the 1980s. These vacationers boosted the country's foreign income by more than $100 million each year.

Photo by Nigel Smith/The Hutchison Library

Aleppo's ancient sites, including one of its many mosques, attract visitors from all over the world. Tourism brings much-needed foreign currency into the country.

The open-air theater at Palmyra is a favorite destination for travelers to this Roman-era city. With its long and mixed history, Syria has much to offer the modern world.

Popular destinations for travelers include Damascus, Aleppo, and Palmyra. Each of these places contains buildings and other artifacts from Syria's past. Damascus and Aleppo feature elements from the Islamic and crusader periods, while Palmyra reflects life during the Roman era.

The Future

At the beginning of the 1980s, Syria stood on the brink of steady economic and social growth. Warfare, costly military spending, and drought hampered the nation's plans. Agricultural output dropped, and Syria spent precious funds on importing food. The nation's oil income rose and fell throughout the decade, and the Assad regime assigned large portions of the country's earnings to defense.

As Syria looks toward the twenty-first century, its leaders will be addressing the problems of economic decline, rapid population growth, and internal disunity. As other Middle Eastern nations explore new avenues to peace in the region, Syria must define the role it wants to play in Arab affairs. The country's decisions will affect not only Syria's future, but the future of the entire Middle East.

Index

64